THE RADIATION SONNETS

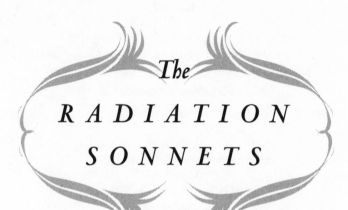

The
RADIATION
SONNETS

For My Love, in Sickness and in Health

by Jane Yolen

ALGONQUIN BOOKS OF CHAPEL HILL 2003

I want to thank everyone involved at the Division of
Radiation Oncology at Bay State Medical Center in Springfield,
Massachusetts, for being caring, nurturing, understanding,
and brilliant professionals.

Published by
Algonquin Books of Chapel Hill
Post Office Box 2225
Chapel Hill, North Carolina 27515-2225

a division of
Workman Publishing
708 Broadway
New York, New York 10003

Library of Congress Cataloging-in-Publication Data
Yolen, Jane.
The radiation sonnets / by Jane Yolen.—1st ed.
p cm.
ISBN 1-56512-402-2
1. Cancer—Patients—Family relationships—Poetry.
2. Cancer—Radiotherapy—Poetry.   3. Married people—Poetry.
4. Sonnets, American.   I. Title.
PS3575.O43R36 2003
811'.54—dc21   2003052013

10   9   8   7   6   5   4   3   2   1
First Edition

Contents

❧

The Beginning . . .

IN JANUARY, AFTER ALMOST A YEAR of pain, an MRI showed an inoperable cancerous tumor in my husband's skull. According to the doctors, radiation was his best hope. But it took another month and a half—days filled with CAT scans, more MRIs, difficult surgical biopsies, and trekking from specialist to specialist (nineteen in all) between Northampton and Boston—before radiation finally began.

According to the doctors, this was hardly any time at all. For the two of us it seemed an eternity.

An eternity. With that metaphor, we plunged into the idea of treatment as poetry.

Once radiation started, I began a sonnet sequence, writing one poem each evening. It was a way to sort through my emotions while holding myself to a difficult task. In fact it was the only thing in my day I seemed to have any control over. For me it was unthinkable to look straight on the possibility of Death without poetic discourse. As Mark Van Doren once wrote: "Wit is the only wall between us and the dark."

Soon, each evening after David was safely in bed, the attic, which I had long ago claimed as my writing room, became my poetic sanctuary. There, in the attic, I poured out my feelings onto the page. About halfway through the forty-three days of treatment, I found myself dreaming in rhyme.

I HAD NOT WRITTEN more than a sonnet or two since college. Most of my published poetry has been either for children or for genre publications or, as one famous poet/editor friend had witheringly pronounced them, *performance* poems, meaning—I suppose—they read well aloud. I have always been wary of the poetry of personal pain, leery of self-exposure. But I did not choose the form, it chose me.

The sonnets not only reflect what happened on a particular day, they also chart my mood at the time. So some of the poems are prayerful, some angry, some despairing, some silly, some full of hope. They speak of naps and nausea, of hair loss and weight loss, of family visits, of friends who volunteer to help, and even of the wrong guidance we received about David's diet. For those who have suffered through cancer or who have been the caregivers for cancer patients, these are familiar-enough subjects.

What is different here is that all these concerns are written about in sonnets, fourteen rhymed lines—with three quatrains and a couplet that sums up the whole. Classical sonnets are in iambic pentameter, a term that explains the number of stresses and syllables in a particular poetic line. But there are as many kinds of sonnets as there are poets making them. Mine varied within the forty-three days I was writing them because my emotions varied. Indeed, you might say these are "radiated" sonnets, changed by the moods that struck me each evening.

Because the compression of poetry echoes the compression of emotion, it was perfect for my needs. I didn't know it then, when I was feverishly writing these sonnets, though I know it now a year later: I needed to hold myself in tightly to get us all through those difficult days. I only cried three times during that ordeal: once when talking on the phone to my daughter-in-law who is a nurse, once when talking to the hospital's social worker, and once when a dear friend put her arms around me and we wept together.

The cancer battle rarely leaves room or time for mourning. We are fighters. We take as our motto the old adage that one does not measure the shroud before the corpse is at hand.

So this book of sonnets is dedicated to David Stemple: husband, partner, lover, father, grandfather, scientist, bird-watcher, bird recordist, golfer, antique collector, "the man who knows everything" according to his nieces and nephews, and a soul of great humor and courage.

THE RADIATION SONNETS

Day 1

A Promise to Eurydice

Do not go, my love—oh, do not leave so soon
Familiar halls and rooms that know your touch.
I want another April, May, and June,
I want—oh still the wanting is so much.
What—forty years gone by? Why need we more
When those before us fill us both with dread?
Oft times I see you staring out the door
As though you're longing for the path ahead.
We go then, hand in hand, into the deep,
Each day a visit to the blank machines.
Those promises we made we mean to keep,
By these mechanicals or other means.
And if alone you chance that endless track,
I'll bring you home, without once looking back.

Day 2

SECOND DAY

If God upon the second day
Had looked askance at His creation,
Sending forth, instead, a ray
To touch all with foul emanation,
Would we think this choice was wise,
Thanking him in song and rhyme?
Would we praise him to the skies
And send our payment in on time?
If doctors see themselves this way,
It does not mean that we have to.
If we must kneel and we must pray,
It's better to the You-Know-Who.
I pray to you, my good old man.
To heal yourself as best you can.

Day 3

Who are you now, so filled with rays
Of death? Have your emotions changed?
I count more precious all our days
While life itself feels rearranged.
Can X rays transubstantiate
A soul, a heart, a love, a life?
Are new emotions given weight?
Are you still husband, I still wife?
I hover, treat you like a child,
I chivy you to eat your meals.
You distance with a look so mild.
Each worries what the other feels.
So constant is the changing tide
Where sea and shore and time collide.

Day 4

The damned machine has broken, cracked,
We prisoners sent back to cell
Still worrying when we'll be wracked,
And if next time we'll bear it well.
In this small moment of relief
We pray the cancer will not grow;
Or, if unfolding like a leaf,
It takes its growing long and slow.
Oh, what a pair, who tremble whether
Torture's done or it is not,
Who count on such a cruel endeavor
To give us all the life we've got.
We cling before the gallows pole
Accepting each the martyr's role.

Day 5

HANGED MAN

They place a mask upon your head,
Like one a hanged man might have known,
And lay you down upon a bed
That's slightly softer than a stone.
You tell me this, your old voice hushed,
Your new voice hoarse in execution.
I doubt that any larynx crushed
Could make so soft an elocution.
The hanged man in the prime tarot
Invests in changing, sacrifice;
So upside down means letting go,
At least as I read his advice.
Still who would trust a life to odds
In decks of cards or hands of gods?

Day 6

A Daughter's Visit

She has your nose, she has your chin,
She has my eyes, my hair.
So if you lose, I still can win
And keep you close and near.
I stare at her, she stares at you
When sleep, that smaller death,
Corrupts your face and takes you to
A world without a breath.
She and I, we breathe as one,
Cadencing the future count.
She's my blood, and she's my bone,
Measuring each small amount
As if we'd breath enough to share
To give you, love, along with care.

Day 7

She takes your working room in hand,
Creating order as she goes,
This child who, in another land,
Had littered her own room with clothes.
And as she organizes things—
By stacking boxes, sorting mess—
Upon the tape a strange bird sings,
An odd lament to our distress.
You sit and watch her at her task,
While nodding judgments from your chair.
Who is this paragon? I ask,
And then remove myself from there,
For she brings order to it all,
Which wraps around you like a shawl.

Day 8

SUCKING CANDIES

One small hard stone, shaped like a tear

Has brought you such relief;

How strange that anything so mere

Can save you from much grief.

My love, I'll buy up carloads,

I'll stash them in our drawers.

I'll memorize the bar codes.

I'll hang them on the doors.

This miracle, this rare device,

So small, so sure, so sweet:

I pray its magic will work twice,

Its mystery repeat,

Or else some new cure can be found

To beat your symptoms to the ground.

Day 9

Mapping the Skull

Another day, another scan.
How well mapped is your skull.
The hemispheres are plotted full,
Both north and south. How then, can
Any traveler make her way
Across your cartographic lawn?
This which was once my sole domain
Is charted, graphed-out, planned, and drawn.
What once was lush is arid, sere,
And yet the noted sculpture stands.
See—I can put my warming hands
Above your forehead, here—and here—
So that on this dear ruined head
I map a drive that's not yet dead.

Day 10

A Little Sleep

A little sleep, a little death,
This first exhaustion frightens me.
I watch, I count each shallow breath,
My prayer a short soliloquy.
You fight the feeling, stay awake,
Your eyes the faded blue of fall,
Refusing for the prayer's sake
To contemplate a nap at all.
This foolish fight is yours to lose.
Just close your eyes, let all pride go.
A moment's sleep's no loss to choose;
I wonder that you feel it so.
Just for a little while please sleep
And like an angel, watch I'll keep.

Day 11

CONFUSION

Have we gone down a winding path,
Dead-ending where we should not be?
Have we been taught wrongheaded math,
Are one and one not two but three?
Nutritionists may differ, sure,
But whom to trust your caring to?
More meetings that we must endure
Just to be told we must undo,
Unpack, unspin, unsnarl, unmoor
Ourselves from past decisions made.
The foods of which we once were sure
Are shown to be a false charade.
If I could know that it was best,
I'd feed you, husband, at my breast.

Day 12

FOOD WARS: FIRST SHOT

Today you did not want to eat.
We knew this day would come.
I tried with fruit and eggs and meat.
You hardly ate a crumb.
The food wars start, with such small shot;
A cannonade comes soon.
You take but little, I give a lot.
You are the victim, I the goon,
The mafioso, Nazi, czar;
I torture you with a stalk
Of celery or caviar.
We war on food where we should talk.
Let's just shake hands and make a truce,
Then speak of terms—over a juice.

Day 13

GOING FOR A RIDE

You, who always drove, are now the rider;

I, who napped on rides, now stay awake.

You, who were the leader, guide, and strider,

Now must close your eyes for your health's sake.

How can we exist with this reversal,

Driving out of Hatfield the wrong way?

Is this some bizarre life-end rehearsal

That we will have to suffer day by day?

Grasp it, live the moment, learn to love it;

Find the humor in our trading roles,

Else we have to scream to God to shove it

As we scoot around these new potholes.

Remember, as we leap this final gap,

At least *you* get to read the bloody map!

Day 14

Like a general left standing in the field,
You count the damage, then you sum the cost.
What matter if peripherals are lost?
What matters is what radiations yield.
The main goal is still the final shrinking
Of the tumor squatting deadly in your skull.
The cost of battle never measures null.
The final price of all this easy drinking
Of life's increasing dismal pricey wine:
Left eyesight missing, cheek unhinged, or deaf ear—
What can you gracefully let disappear?
The choice is neither yours nor is it mine.
So Braveheart let us damn the damnable cost.
As long as there is life, then all's not lost.

Day 15

Work Week

Here's Monday, our old enemy, old friend.
We workers rise and take our rising slow.
Then trudging to the graveyard shift, we go
To view again a workweek without end.
Real workers wait on Fridays for their wages;
Each moment on the treadmill counts toward pay.
But you, tied to machinery each workday,
Have only flesh and blood to be your gauges.
So Monday, here we are again, unwilling,
Yet knowing that the week ends with a check
Of eye and ear, of temple, jaw and neck,
A complication of this kind of billing.
We take our wallets out to pay the bill
With grace and optimism—and good will.

Day 16

TALISMAN

The first time down, we saw him in the grass,
Flagged by the white breast, the broad brown wings.
Now we count on him each time we pass,
Our talisman, mascot. What luck he brings
We cannot know yet, not for weeks and weeks.
We must endure your sores, your aches, your pains,
Your quiet separation, your midday peaks,
And the guarded optimism at your gains.
What does the hawk mean? Nothing more
Than a buteo on the hunt in a field.
Yet each day if we don't see him before
Your radiation starts, we want to yield,
To turn around, run home, our journey done,
Our talisman fled, and all good luck gone.

Day 17

Food Wars: Second Front

The war proceeds, the mines are laid;
We glare across the battle lines.
This deadly game that must be played
Of when and how the patient dines.
I buy supplies, you bomb the best
With careless strikes of scattered shot.
I try to tempt you with the rest:
One day it's soup, the next it's not.
And so I fill these warring days,
Oft eating both meals by myself.
The fridge groans with your castaways.
Good soldiers rot upon the shelf.
The line between our troops now blurs.
In war we take no prisoners.

Day 18

Letting Go

A friend drove you today, I did not go.
An ache remains, a pinprick in my breast,
Reminding me just what I ought to know:
The caregiver, as well, still needs her rest.
You laughed with him along the long highway,
He promised that he'd volunteer for more.
I gave him tea, we'd things enough to say,
But deep inside me some unknown piece tore.
Yet in this first pained time we've been apart
I sensed, my dear, an infinite rehearsal:
A gap, a hole, a pinpoint in my heart,
A space for which I fear there's no reversal.
Then help me, love, to sigh and let you go,
If terror, time, and tumor make it so.

Day 19

TEMPLE

Good skull, old skull, I see you today
That once was hidden well by hair,
By mustache, beard, by black, by grey;
What now is reddened, once was fair.
Good skull, old skull, I touch the skin
That's taut across your ruined temple,
Now stretched fine and parchment thin,
The known, the loved, the David Stemple.
Here craters gape where once was grass,
Great tumbled rocks and pillars shattered,
Caryatids—then stone, now glass.
Once upon a time that mattered.
But temples fallen can still rise.
There's life yet in those loved blue eyes.

Day 20

RIDE

Off you go again, like a toddler to school,
In a neighbor's car for a noonday ride;
Free at last from the tyrant's rule,
Free of the house where there's nowhere to hide.
And here I stay, feeling guilty and lost,
Feeling scared and panicked, yet glad you've gone.
The caregiver rarely counts her own cost;
Even more rarely is she left alone.
I hold you close, and I push you away,
Dream of funerals and letting go.
But it's for miracles I pray each day,
While working hard to make it so.
Then, like any mother nervously at home,
I stand watch at the window until you come.

Day 21

We're not dancing at the Irish Fest today,
Nor clapping for our son's wild band.
This was not where we'd expected to stay,
Not quite the holiday we had planned.
Our calendars have all been changed,
Dates struck off, erased, removed;
Parties missed and travel rearranged,
Our lifetime plotting suddenly disproved.
We no longer live year by year,
Nor month by month, nor day by day,
But meal by meal—or so you fear—
And never far from the pills dare stray.
Still soon—whatever *soon* implies—
We'll have all the time that love still buys.

Day 22

PENULTIMATE

This penultimate week, this Ferris wheel
Which, hand in hand, we sit atop,
Here in this moment before the squeal
That signals the final perilous drop;
Beneath us people unheeding go,
Above us birds in the hundreds sing.
Children play on the ground below.
The gondola begins its languid swing.
Do we trust the driver of the wheel,
Or fear the bolts will suddenly sever?
Or do we, here in the air, just kneel
And pray that we might go together?
Hold my hand, love, as we fly
Downward to the earth from sky.

Day 23

EXPECTATIONS

Our youngest son flew in this night,
The one that under my heart I carried
Some eight years after we were married.
He spoke of the brutal and bumpy flight.
In his eyes a certain new fear waited;
Not, I am sure, for the plane's delays,
But in keeping with these most dismal days,
For what he thought was upstairs, fated.
When we tiptoed into the close bedroom,
Your eyes flew open, your familiar smile
Told him his coming was worth each mile
He had crossed to find you in this tomb.
We fear dying changes the living,
And that we've nothing worth the giving.

Day 24

You've not been beardless in forty years.

Luxuriant growth becomes your face.

Yet hair loss, despite my many fears,

Has not the mighty ship displaced.

I see your neck now, and your chin,

Though weaker than I had remembered.

But still the keel's kept taut by skin

And overall the ship's well-timbered.

Prow of nose, now prouder still,

Rising from the hairless cheeks.

The doctors promise your hair will

Be growing back in several weeks.

Let me this new vessel know a bit

Before its sides must be refit.

Day 25

WAITING ROOM

Let me now speak of the waiting room,
That outer chamber, that gate to hell,
More like a motel than a tomb,
Where a faint antiseptic smell
Invades the bleak halls. This is not
A place of fun, where Disneys go.
It is neither too cold nor too hot.
The TV blares some inane show.
And we who wait do not converse,
We do the crossword, read a book.
As if the very act is cursed,
We hardly even share a look.
We do not smile, yet glow with health.
Our secret shame, and our only wealth.

Day 26

Do we know yet of death or fate?
No seer, it seems, can tell us so:
The final call, the terminal date,
The moment when you'll have to go?
I would not shut the gate quite yet,
But guardedly will keep it wide
And with a heavy boot that's set
Against the jamb, keep you outside.
When we began this endless trek,
I feared I saw a darkened door,
Through which a line of marching sick
Were heading for some winter shore.
But now the news the doctor brings
Seems to promise other springs.

Day 27

An Additional Week of Radiation

What's a week, my love, more or less?
Another five rays sent through the bone,
Another chance for the doctor to guess
If the tumor has shrunk or if it's grown.
What's a week, my love, but seven days
To think of living, not think of death?
Seven more days, that's seven more ways
To try and take another breath.
What's a week, my dear, but a bit more time
To love, to live, to still just *be*?
Seven more tries to make a rhyme.
Seven more days there is a "we."
This unsuspected new decision
Plays havoc with my keen addition.

Day 28

A Bad Day

One bad day in ten, I can't complain,
Though it's a misery to see you low.
I count each wince, each groan, each pain,
I counsel you, as if I know
What food or ointment, potion or pill
Can turn the tide. I wade into the wave,
Like old Canute trying to stop the spill,
To make the ocean of agony behave.
If I could make the swim for you, I would.
Instead I hold the towel to rub you down.
I'd take the plunge in your stead if I could,
Or hand in hand we both could drown.
Still, this wet wilderness of pain
Will tomorrow be dry again.

Day 29

FOOD WARS: THIRD FRONT

You have dubbed me the Food Dominatrix.
I have ordered the boots and the whip.
Would that there were so easy a fix
To your food aversions as this small quip.
I've laid siege to the shelves of the grocery,
Looking for edibles tempting you to eat.
I've bankrupted my personal treasury
Trying fruit and Jell-O and soup and meat.
Far easier to tie your wrists to the bed,
Far easier to whip you into submission,
Far easier to stuff your resisting head
Than to ask and never receive permission.
So on with the boots; boy, hand me the quirt.
Here is the entrée. There's the dessert.

Day 30

Changing the Angle

What a rare geometry is this,
Another entrance for the deadly rays.
So acute this new angle, set to miss
The corner of the eye, it does amaze
Us both. Oh, if such relations
Could be guaranteed as true.
We could take our geometric stations
And from there admire the view.
I fear this angle as all the rest,
Will bring you nothing but extra pain.
It's a shift of focus, another test,
But geometry deceives us once again.
We need, I guess, angels, and not angles,
The first one saves, the other merely mangles.

Day 31

Daffodil Day

The techs all gave out daffodils
To everyone they zapped today,
Surely a much better way
To enhance health than pills,
Or rays, or the occasional leeching.
The dafs are still folded tight,
As if unfurling their flags might
Have seemed overreaching
In that blank hospital room.
But now, standing up to their knees
In water, trying to please
Onlookers, they positively bloom.
I wish a day of soaking feet
All your medical needs could meet.

Day 32

JOURNALING

Our daughter and granddaughter write in journals:
Thoughts, rubbings, the minutiae of their days,
The beginnings of paintings, stampings; the kernels
Of poetry, adages, Post-its—the latest craze.
I am too old, too tired, too focused on illness
To take up journaling, despite their delight.
My thoughts and rubbings bend only toward wellness.
One poem alone at bedtime completes my night.
If in another lifetime, all tumors behind,
I have energy and time for joyous creation,
All of our friends will then surely find
Me journaling in daily celebration.
Until that moment, one poem maintains.
A tight compression alone sustains.

Day 33

ONE MORE WEEK

There is something Alpine about this day.
We stand on the precipice, gaze into the mist.
One more week you must suffer the ray.
Let's be careful in descending not to twist
An ankle, a knee, to add to our woes.
Just a smooth road running down from the peak.
Metaphor can't chart how this trip goes.
One more week! Just one more week!
And then I remember, that extra day,
A substitute for the session we skipped.
Suddenly the week takes on a new array,
A color unspecified, a muscle ripped.
How can a single day seem so long
And make our descent go so damned wrong?

Day 34

ESCAPE

Escaping from the house of pain,
I take my granddaughter into town.
The sky alternates first sun, then rain,
As pathetic a fallacy as one could own.
Coincidence in life is seen as hallowed,
Haloed, miraculous, goddess graced.
In art such weather is not allowed,
But edited out, deleted, erased.
Should I then read entrails, cast the bones,
Check our palms, or throw the sticks,
Rearrange the future stones,
Or any other sacred tricks?
Or just come home, refreshed, renewed,
Like Humpty Dumpty, wholly glued?

Day 35

BIRD-WATCHING

The birder goes once again to the woods,
The sites and sounds of his delight.
Weakened, still on liquidized foods,
He takes his granddaughter to watch the flight
Of hawk and dove and phoebe in the grass.
They mark their books, they talk of birds.
She helps to make the hard day pass,
She gives him more than comforting words;
She gives him back his sense of worth,
His old strength, which I take away,
So worried about his lessening girth
Or the loss of hair totaled day by day.
There's nothing so strengthening than to be told
That you are a god by a seven-year-old.

Day 36

April Fools

To the outside world, we are April fools,
Hoping for miracles, believing in none.
Intellect, science, hard facts are our tools,
Which we will believe in till treatment is done.
You've read up on cancers, medicines, the lot;
I've queried doctors, acquaintances, friends.
We know what there is, and what there is not,
All the alphas/omegas, beginnings/ends.
And yet . . . and yet, when you are not aware,
I've gotten down on my aching old knees
Offering up a nonbeliever's prayer.
If there *is* a God, surely He/She accepts these.
Foxholes, airplanes, cancer makes us kin
To those for whom prayer is the place to begin.

Day 37

FOOD WARS: FOURTH FRONT

You who are sixty have just turned six:
You dissemble, deceive, eat half, call it whole.
Soon you will dump the contents of the bowl
As part of your latest bag of tricks.
I'm mother now, measuring, making you eat,
Counting the sips, teaspoons, doses, bites.
Your half smile diffuses all our fights,
As you whisper the magic word, "Replete."
I who never resisted you cannot now learn;
I set the soup before you, then move away,
Hoping a stronger hunger on another long day
Will bring you to table, will help you return
To find the miracle that fine food brings,
Along with salt, sex, and other good things.

Day 38

Words

There is one word we have not spoken: *Death.*
We are experts in circumlocution:
"Passing over," "morbidity," "loss of breath,"
"Worst-case scenario," "execution."
We say you're "unwell" and "under the gun,"
That you have a problem in your head.
All those words to get around the one,
That single syllable too awful to be said.
Why invest one noun with our worst fears,
That dreamscape figure from darkest night?
To even think it brings me to tears,
Before I have to say it, I'll take flight.
But Death, the subject and object of our speech,
Is the one true word that lies within our reach.

Day 39

Now for a moment let's consider the tongue,
That seat of language, that soul of wit,
That place where food now tastes like dung,
Where the aftertaste is often shit.
I cannot grasp this evolution—
Wine to vinegar, milk to mud.
I fight to win the revolution
Without our spilling too much blood.
Your mouth hangs open, full of sores,
The wounds of battles in the past.
I buy you mouthwash in the stores
And pray the aching will not last.
Still, now with victory in our sights,
I've no more stomach for these fights.

Day 40

HAWKS

So let us in this last long stoop,
Like a hawk on its unwary prey,
Separate ourselves from the group
Who fear we will not carry the day.
Let us leap up with flaring wings,
Sail off into the rising dawn,
Embrace the warmth the new sun brings,
And catch the wind before it's gone.
We can be broad-winged and soaring,
Light against the lightening sky.
Loose the jesses, leave the mooring,
And love once more before we die.
For like the birds that mate for life,
I am yours, the hawk's true wife.

Day 41

VISITORS

When I am near, you fall asleep.
Is this a compliment or not?
When visitors arrive, you keep
Them entertained, as if you've got
Some minor ailment, just a cold,
And not a tumor in your head.
You look so young again, not old,
Alive when you had looked new dead.
If I believed you could be cured
By these old friends just stopping by,
Then all the days of pain endured
Would seem a crime, a joke, a lie.
But how I loved your laughing face
Which did the last weeks' pains erase.

Day 42

Away

All the way to New Hampshire I feel a pain
Beneath my breast, not heartburn, not that,
But fear that I will not see you again.
Like some cowardly, ill-mannered rat
I have left the rusting, half-sunken boat,
Deserting before you go down for good.
Calling home between speeches, I note
You did not eat, though I left much food.
I don't sleep well, worried about your sleep.
Much too distracted, too ill-prepared,
I wonder — with me gone — who will keep
You company, make meals, care as I cared.
And then I return, earlier than meant,
To find you sleeping, after birding, utterly spent.

Day 43

GRADUATION DAY

On this final day, this graduation,
From the harrowing halls of treatment,
From the harsh teachings of radiation,
Burning as learning (or so the heat meant)
You hold out toward me your secret mask,
That sculpted instrument of torture.
I accept it without being asked,
This relic of the cancer culture.
How could I know what went on inside
That hidden, that forbidden room,
Where your skull lay opened wide
To the rays' ever more deadly perfume?
The mask keeps hidden what we most fear.
All I know now is that you are still here.

And After . . .

Is there an after?

Actually, there is a next day and a next and the one after that. We cannot say the word "cured" for the tumor is still squatting in David's skull, beaten back for the moment, quiet, and like Brer Fox, laying low. It has not moved or changed in nine months, a dark gestation period. But still, it is inarguably and palpably there.

One year later, normal life for all of us has resumed, but at a quieter pace. Our grandson was born several months after radiation was completed, and he was named David after my husband—which brought us all to tears. Our daughter and her daughters live with us now, reuniting the generations. Our youngest son's wife had twin daughters in May. There is a wonderful forward movement in all this begetting, and David revels in it.

We still look for the red-tailed hawk, our talisman, whom we named Adeno, each time we pass through his territory. When he is not there, I think my heart stutters.

The scans every three months—and now six months —have become routine but are never approached without some measure of fear. We know this is a knife's edge. If I ask David how he is feeling, he is quick to give me a run-down of symptoms. Vigilance has become part of our everyday existence. We are not counting on sharing another forty years together. But then were we ever? We have both outlived each of our mothers' life spans already. It doesn't take an actuarial table to tell us we are on borrowed time. Only now, we are painfully aware of how few years may be left and it has made the moments even more precious.

Eating is still a problem. For a year we counted on honey-banana-strawberry milk shakes to maintain David's caloric intake. Recently has the dentist been able to work on a bridge that links David's few remaining teeth. Radiation in the skull compromises the jawbone. The lack of saliva— another by-product of radiation in that area—makes false teeth difficult if not impossible.

Still there are some good signs. The bridge is hold-ing. I call it the Bridge of Size, because I hope it helps build him up again. For the most part, the taste buds have returned and at the latest doctor's visit, some saliva was spotted as well. I envy David his svelte figure but would hate to lose weight that way. Salads may be a thing of the past for him; they are difficult to process, impossible to chew. But each week he rediscovers an old edible friend, so we are not ruling out salad greens entirely. The food wars continue, but it is a cold war. We both know the rules.

WHEN I FINISHED THE SONNETS, I asked David if he wanted to read them. He has always been a careful editor of my work. Wisely, he decided not to. Our daughter, who reads everything I write, made that "mistake"—so she calls it—and cannot bring herself to read them again. She wept till her eyes were raw and red. The poems brought back those days too strongly for her.

I asked David how he would feel if I took some of the poems to my writers' group. They had each come over with food during the weeks of radiation. Leslea's grandmother's chicken soup was the best. He allowed me to read the poems to my "literary ladies." It was the group's instant critical assessment that drove me to send the sonnets—again with David's permission—to my agent. She and her assistant demanded they be sent on to publishers. David, without a single demur, agreed. He said, "Those poems are *you*." And we both felt that if they could help others. . . .

That the book found an editor seemed one more miracle in a year of hard miracles.

"I promise to be around for publication day," David told us.

We are all holding him to that promise.

—JANE YOLEN

Phoenix Farm, spring 2003

Jane Yolen is the author of the best-selling children's books *How Do Dinosaurs Say Good Night?*, *How Do Dinosaurs Get Well Soon?*, *Owl Moon*, *The Devil's Arithmetic*, and many other modern classics. *Newsweek* dubbed her "the Hans Christian Andersen of America" and the *New York Times* called her "a modern equivalent of Aesop." Her books have been awarded the Caldecott Medal, two Christopher Awards, the Regina Medal, the Sydney Taylor Book Award, two Nebula Awards, a Society of Children's Book Writers award, and she was a National Book Award finalist, among many other honors. She has been given three honorary doctorates for her body of work.

Dr. David Stemple was for many years a professor of computer science at the University of Massachusetts, Amherst. The last four years he was at the university, he served as chairman of the department. Upon retiring, he became a full-time bird recordist, traveling through the USA, South and Central America, and the British Isles recording birds, working on scientific analysis of his data, and donating the recordings to the Macaulay Library of Natural Sounds at Cornell University.

The couple lives in Massachusetts and Scotland. They have three children and six grandchildren. A portion of the proceeds from *The Radiation Sonnets* will go to the Division of Radiation Oncology at Bay State Medical Center in Springfield, Massachusetts, where David Stemple was treated.

More information can be found at www.janeyolen.com.